Elements

Aislyn de Witt

BookLeaf Publishing

India | USA | UK

Presentation by *BookLeaf Publishing*

Web: www.bookleafpub.com

E-mail: info@bookleafpub.com

ISBN:

First edition 2022

Elements

Earth and water
Create mud
Water and Air
Create ice
Fire and Sand
Make glass
Clay needs to be fired
To be fortified
But what creates man?
Are we created when we meet our other half?
Separated by the heavens above to leave us
Alone
Defenceless
Did the heavens create my flesh?
Or the Earth?
Or my Mother?
And does it meanless
If I don't know?

Earth

The day I was born still lives in me
Ground into the fibre of my bones
Coursing through my veins
So a curious man walks in one day
And asks me my age
A rude question certainly
I tell him of the fire in the sky
The floods that crashed into my Mother
The thick mud that caked my face
and tried to choke me
That my mother saved me from drowning
That she willed herself to stand the fire
To heat her through
Til she knew I was safe
That her strength hardened my bones
That the fire failed in its task
My mother never knew about the cracks
The fractures of my bones
Where seeds stayed dormant
For only a short time
Then grew with careful
Exploration
I told him the truth
That these cracks make me love
Love my bones

Love my mother
Love my world all the more
For my short-lived term
Besides who can say if life is better
Than life
Perhaps one day my Jason will come
Will make an army from my scattered
Bones
With the fierceness of loyalty
And the strength of love
The curious man knew not what to do with this
I can say he did not like my tale
Or perhaps liked it so much
That he felt the need to take my arm
My precious bones
And crack open the contents
And that day he showed me
That the day I was born
Will be a day never forgotten

Air

The world began with a kiss
Two lips parted and in that wisp of air
The universe
Exploded in the openness of the void
And in the welcome warmth
Of soft embrace
Brought forth the life of millions
One-touch
One simple touch
Held in perpetuity
Til seconds bend to years
As warped as the words used
To define it
The world began with a kiss
It lives in that state
Never touching
But always connected
I started with a kiss
Perchance I'll end with one too

Water

I looked directly into the sun
And the golden embers blinded me
I was waiting for you to come
I was hoping that you would find me
I watched, and waited, and hoped
And hid as best I could
The girl who just couldn't cope
And never did as she should
The sun was blistering and hot
My skin scorched and was burnt
For things I knew were not
But soon I'd sense your embrace
And feel my loneliness churn
For love denies what is base
And truly when will I learn
Yet
Feeling the brush of your hair
Can truly intoxicate
But you made a choice and swore
That my place and yours were out
Beyond the bounds of War
And how long may I still doubt
When your hand remains in mine
I looked directly into the sun
You sat beside me this time

Fire

I burn like a fire
It's inescapable.
The scorching flame
That may escape
And envelope this form.
A mass of burning flesh
But for now
It beats within my chest.
Upon my checks
It seeks to burrow.
Through my stretching skin
Like a heart that bursts
And paints the wall technicolor.
Til it becomes red
All red
From the root
To my head
A sticky body
Drenched in sweat
And gold til
Phoenix-like reemergence.
To some better life
A world of hope
And love and joy

Except I chose
To burn it to the floor
So here I burn
Majestic
But really just
For a moment

Wood

When you look at a tree, what do you see?
When you're inspecting its gnarled knot-work,
Caressing its cool mahogany skin.
What is it that you're looking for?
 You used to talk to me about fairy gardens.
I suppose you wouldn't remember.

You were five or six then. You were so particular
Telling me these tales.
Because "not all trees are solid dad… did you
know that?
Sometimes you greet this old friend and you fall
through the edges."
You were so emphatic, so proud you knew
something I didn't.

Your mum used to tell me such similar things. I
think you got it from her.
She used to tell me about the fabric that lined the
inside of trees.
 That it was pure gold,
"Wouldn't it be far more interesting if it were?"
Every "friend" we encountered in the park must
be inspected

Touch it to your tongue,
She would say
Taste the gold, just like the old diggers.
And as we walked the block before her flat on
repeat
 Delaying the inevitable of me dropping her off
at the door,
 She'd tell me that those golden threads
They ran from tree to tree,
Well they ran from her to me.

I suppose darling that means they run between
us too.
I don't think we ever told you, but your mother
made your crib.
Twenty weeks pregnant I might add.
I don't think the millers had ever been so
shocked by a sight.
This little woman wondering about the site in a
pair of overalls
A belly about half her size.
But it had to be the right tree you see.
You had to have the right tree.
She would say "it's the earths gift"
And a mothers

She would just laugh.
It was certainly an interesting experience,

Your mother waking me up at 4am with power
tools,
Your crib was ready by the time that you were.
She was besotted with you the first few months.

 One day she came home from taking you to the
park,
she said you'd both decided which path to turn
onto by hugging the trees.
You really loved to play together, but suddenly
you ran over to the swings and told her
she "had to listen more carefully, otherwise
you'll only hear what you want to".
 It was that day that she started this.

 I know it seems small
 And there are a few more
But she was most proud of this one.
 It's made from the branches of your crib

When you trace your fingers along it,
Rubbing the lines of each carved feather,
All those threads,
That have been with us all this time, in repeated
blocks,
And stolen kisses and swinging higher than
before,
They'll come to life, and she'll know all of our
stories."

Don't think you thought your ol' dad could be
romantic before this eh?
I know it's not blue,
hardly seems borrowed to return to you
something that was always yours,
but I thought it could count.
She took the carved cardinal and thought it an
odd choice,

As she ran her fingers up the delicately carved
lines of the beak the threads illuminated, and
suddenly she understood.

Steel

I wish I could just die
Dry out the morsels of pain
That solid membrane impermeable
Weep out til solid mass remains
Removing trembling husk
Til salt tears form salt mass
Eroded by the sea
Dried out, and emptying daily
Til pure essence remains
And husk becomes unseen
Unremembered save salt tears
Dripping into quivering mouths
Clasping for breath that hopes
Should never come
Waiting for the finite
Til cold slab of granite
lies in bed, and questions
Who is the imposter?

Clay

I gave you hope when it was clear you needed it
I gave you trust when yours was broken
I gave you faith when my trust ran out
I gave my love, endlessly and unreservedly
But when I needed it the most I had given it all
away
And when I had nothing you were nowhere in
sight
But the clay left in my pocket
Run through fingers and through earth
And I made so much happiness
That an empty heart could burst

Mud

Petrified
Fingers trembling
With such intensity that my body shakes
My nails cracked in dirt
Maybe it's skin
I don't know anymore
Am I breathing?
I need to remember to do that
I forgot
With your touch
I forgot
To breath
I suppose I mean my body forgot
Was it your touch?
Or the wall?
The doctors said wood
Was that the bed?
My table?
I love your touch
I shouldn't say that
I don't love
I love you
I shouldn't say that
I don't think I can go back

No
Yes I know
No not you
The place
I guess I mean my home
My bed
My table
My wall
My sheets so tightly pressed to my head
It was an accident
I said it was an accident
You didn't have to lie
Well why would you
You weren't there I suppose
Were you there?
No, no
I knew that
Why are my fingers?
Are you okay
I'm sorry
I'm sorry I wouldn't hurt you
It was instinct
I didn't mean
Please
Please forgive me
You don't have to
I know you don't have to
But I promise I will make it better
I shouldn't say that

I should leave
I shouldn't stay
My fingers keep trembling
Like I'm afraid
I know I'm not
I can handle anything
That's what everyone says
I should wash my hands
But they're caked
I don't know how
I don't know how
I don't know… anymore

Sand

There is never enough time
Is there?
Is that the secret?
The thing that adults seemed to hide from me
The smirk when I was a child
There is never enough

I don't want to be selfish
Maybe I am
Maybe I am the most selfish thing in the world
A child
I don't want to be a child

I just want more
More time
More moments looking at your face
More afternoons
More evenings to regard you
To spectate at the grace of your movements
The slight sway of your hips
The slant of your wrist as you press a wax seal
And the flourish of you pouring yourself a drink

Can you tell me why?

Why it feels like sand slipping through my
fingers
Like memories of a distant life
Why?
Do I feel like I lost you before I'm gone?

I want to say it was enough
That the moments of you were enough
That an evening would've been enough
Like I am satiated by our life
But is it enough?
How can I be happy knowing it wasn't
It wasn't enough

That even time travel wouldn't make it enough
That had I known you since birth I would still
beg
Still plead
For just a moment more

I'm selfish
I suppose that I cannot deny
But the sands are almost up
Almost gone my love
So tell me
Can I be enough?

Glass

Solid mass
Hollow space
Splintered face
Shadowed glass

Explosive point
Fractured frame
Cracking pane
space disjointed

Tiny graze
Endless shard
Picture marred
Ego fazed

Married with drops of blood
Eyes frightened from sight
Endless feeling of pulling
Something that may never come out

Twinkle bright
Tiny knives
Scared life
Full of fright

Blink shards
Glass flicked
Glass sticks
Blink away shards

Structure

My eyes are drawn shut
And that's okay for now
I'm trusting you to guide me
As we lie tangled side by side
Your steady heartbeats through
Reverberated through my back
As I move my arm behind my head
And grasp your hand in mine
My toes move down to make you twitch
As the hardness of your jaw tears my neck
And lay bathed in sound
Your hands fall to my stomach
As I pull it to my waist
Avoiding all the fat that's there
Nuzzling into your face
As folk guitar fills the wholesome room
You ask "are you awake"I pull you closer as I
nod
Pulling the rifts from the air
Those golden strumming into us
Til we begin to vibrate at that
Perfect frequency
Of doing everything by nothing
We lie content
Back to chest

"Ow" "you found a knot"
"I'm sorrybaby"
As your finger digs harder
But still, I don't
Turn my head
Just inhaling your aroma
And people have many answers
But I know what's true to me
You smell like the oldest tree
Whose learned they can still bloom
The show moves on
You feel my tears "oh baby are you?"
Instead the reply you get
Is shaking hands pulling your arm
Directly to my heart
It finally ends
And then you ask
Tea? Or bed
As we roll in bobbing synchronicity
My head lands on your chest
A leg wraps over you
"Hello koala" you've replied
And so I nestle into you
To sleep til
We don't have to rise

Reflections

One bottle
Gentle pouring
Flirting giggles
Bursting bubbles
Cute stories
Witty. Speak
Little things to
Make you think
Two bottles
Candlelit
Raising tensions
Deep embraces
Soaring sighs
Raucous laughter
Needs that rise
From green glass
A Chest that
Raises to speak
Holding for another drink
Three bottles
Heaving chests
Breathy sobs
Shaking breasts
Stories drawn
Opening wounds

Drops of blood
Soothe the soul
Pain for pain
Tit for tat
Deep expression
Filled with doubt
Child's trauma
Fucked adult
Lies and truth
Fly with ease
Til their just
The simple bit
Twist the lid
Don't look back
Four bottles
Simple needs
Fish and chips
Cravings plead
Wagers rise
 Pleasured pain
Treasured hurt
Different face
But same words
Four five
Fevered fun
Daring games
Hiccup
Four five
Heaving up

Empty brain
Four five
Feeling pain
Four five
Feeling fine
Four five
Rising up
four five
Don't say no
Four five
Sinking down
Four five
Four five
Four five
5 am
Sleep before 6
Sleep to stop
Sleep to escape
Sleep

Fired

Ginger
Garlic
Stinging the eyes and
Opening the senses
A hearty mix
A gentle fold
Hand over hand and
Doubt eclipsed
With only love there to learn
Aromatic plants and
enigmatic glints
That pulls from the sparkle
From eye to lips
The brazen grin
That sparks contempt
And restorative eye
That soothes as Aloe
And when we say
Hand on hand
With no need to shy
No sense of loss or fear
A simple smile responding
And oh those times
Echo still
With no courtesy to construct

Time and lives blended still
In this familial marriage
Of joy and loss
Of warmth and frost
And I trust these times
Not gone
The echos linger
And mould my life
Allowing all new sense of joy
But in the warm inviting smell
My heart can't help but mourn
I smelled garlic
Wafting through the air
Today of all days
It made me stop
And think I felt
Joy tingle on my tongue
So in the quiet of the noise
I know our love's not gone

Bound

I don't know if I can survive
This whole affair
I worked so hard to just be
But I drown in thinning air
I'm losing the ability
The thing I want the most
Because I'm being drowned
With no lifeguard around
So as I face these problems
The ones of my own making
I wish that I had someone
Who loved me more than destruction
Because pain is so alluring
A friend who can be depended
But that sickly sweet voice
Can fester in an ear
And ask for my destruction
For a single moment of Love
And an addicted body
Craves dependency
The conditional phrase
And I am sick, so sick
That I would open up my veins
So I wish that you still loved me
And held me in your arms

But I don't know if I'll survive this
My love
So we'll say goodbye

Balance

There's a string that runs across the city
I bet you wouldn't know it
It runs above everyones heads
I bet they wouldn't know it
I saw a girl up there once
I was on the way to the train
She was tumbling
A spinner in constant oscillation
I saw her span the city with such speed
I was convinced she was part cat
She didn't look down at me
Her eyes were on the horizon
Not on the ground
Not like the sea of people that walked in time
with me
A mediocre pace set by standardized lights
That would only change if a mouse chewed
through
A green wire in some office somewhere
Or someone wanted to spell 80085 on a
calculator
I'm glad she didn't see me
Not that day
The day I left my life

The day I had to start a new one
The day I felt broken
Because hope was a lie that any fool could see
Maybe I was a fool
But I'm a fool who found you
I found your string
And I'm ready
I think
Well I'm ready to try
So tell me
To start off with
Just simply
Which foot?
Left or right?

Freed

The pain I felt was always mine
For you could never see it
The tears I cried were always mine
For you could never hear it
So when I cried for hope not loss
You were nowhere to be seen
And when I felt her daring kick
Well what's "proven could be seen"
So when I felt the feeling stop
There was death inside you too
And when I needed you the most
To yourself you must be true
So now that I am tired and broke
You've left so you can't see it
And all I have is to try and call
You've turned your phone to silent
An irritation, a past mistake
That you have promptly dealt with
A new life with no risk
You'd rather enter into
I know it's hard to accept being good
So you've left me in the past
I know it's hard to leave your heart open
So you keep me in the dark

Ritual

Today
I walk to the centre of the woods
My pocket is full
I am empty
I walk
Everyday
And leave my gifts
All my gifts
Until my pocket is as empty
Each day a handful
And every day a handful more
I grasp my gifts
Too tight
Til the gift becomes dry
Til my hand starts to crack
Like stones piercing weathered skin
But I keep my course
I leave the gifts
I leave
Everything
Some days the path is harder
Some days the dream grows weary
Each day the gift comes more polluted
The dream polluted
But when I reach the centre of the woods

The road, I know not why I walk
I stop
And I leave
I will my fingers to separate
To unclasp a stony grip
To let just enough air in
That my lungs depress
That I can take one more step
My joints shake
Trembling with the ecstasy of the dream
Weeping with the pain of the dream
When finally a grain falls through
A single fingertip that released its dream
Until all the soil falls
The dream is gone
Still, I revisit the spot
The daily pilgrimage
The walk is harder now
Most things are harder now
I will have to stop for a little while soon
But little feet will rejoin me
Tomorrow

Ignition

Are you okay?
You ask with such tenderness
I could believe you cared
But I know you don't
What's your favourite book?
You would ask
On repeat
Like it was an idle curiosity
Demons
And who is that?
A fair question to be sure
Perhaps a fair question the first four times of
asking
You've asked it over breakfast
The walks to lectures
On drunken nights to lend an air of
intellectualism
A curious question to be sure
Perhaps that is why you persist in the question
Why it is of such dire importance
The forefront of your mind
Perhaps the fact that I love reading of cruelty
being made not born
Well perhaps that gives you some great insight
Almost certainly

What's your favourite book?
You ask over the tea set you bought me
In the bedroom we share
In the shirt I bought you
Demons
By that writer
Yes
By that writer
By that one, I spoke of time and again
By that one that I kept revisiting
By the one that one I read when you would ask others
others
In your most tender voice if
"They were okay"
Perhaps they believe you
Perhaps they think they are the only one
Perhaps they think your words of cruelty some confidence
confidence
A secret you can share
That it's a rarity you speak this way
Perhaps they think their names haven't been named in your cruellest moments
named in your cruellest moments
I wonder
What is their favourite book?
And is that Homer, or Joyce?

Grace

Your first smile
Coincided with the coldest night
You lit up the world
You filled my heart
Flailing limbs
Now a sign of joy
An internal exploration
For the world to enjoy with you

Your humor so intoxicating
That a cackle from you
Would send an army into fits
Of giggles as large as you

Your frustration
Too heartbreaking to watch
To see the world
That we set up and fail in day after day

But in the moments of fear
You remain true
You let my arms wrap around you
And submit your head to my shoulder
Trusting I will put the world to rights

And I will prove you right by finding you in my
arms
Every night
I promise

Your truth would never fault me
Though I know I will fail
I will never leave on a low
I will try again
Until I cannot try any longer

When you want to take charge
It's waiting
But my arms will be within reach
If ever you should need me
For your solitary moments
Your quiet discourse with Winter
Your playful smile with Spring
Your explosive exploration of Summer
And your lectures with Autumn

I will never leave your side
Because you're the one that saved my life
And salvaged my heart.

Light

I used to drink too much
Or so they like to tell me
I would stay out too late
And leave my friends to worry

I would steal the occasional smoke
And use people to define my pleasure
I would deny my conscious
And starve my belly

Cause that's what people use to tell me

I sit alone in the dark
I watch too much crap tv
I let the static buzz through my head
Means I don't have to think

I don't cook all the time
The micro-meal is my friend
I don't do what I love
Some days

Cause if I did they'd never end

I need sleep
I need time
To eat and drink
So I am told

But still, I'd miss what I am needing
If I lived another's tale
I make my own rules
I refuse to make someone happy

Cause all I need is you

That was a song
When I was younger
When my mum kept me wrapped in her arms
And determined my music preferences

But really it is quite true
Guess her taste had some points
I never really noticed what I was missing
Til you came into my life

Cause I didn't want to miss you

I spend every day missing you
Enchanted by you
Infuriated and mad
But the commonality is you

Because you made it all worth it
Though I don't think I should tell you
You have a big enough head
I shouldn't inflate it

Cause I'm supposed to help you

That's my job
A star landed in my letterbox
And sent me the papers to sign
That's my job

I said it when I met you
I wept into your arms
I'm sorry if I ever hurt you
Or neglected what you need

Cause I believe you belong here, with me

And you're not allowed to argue with me
You'll never know how dark the world was
From the times before you were here
I hope you never have to see

I hope your light keeps us rising
Makes us better than we were
I hope that love defines us
Not the hate that lives in hearts

Cause I just wanna protect you

From myself
From the world
From yourself
When you need it

So tell me, sir
What do you think?
Park
Or pool?

Cause I wanna know you